Interview Season

A Business Student's
Guide to a Dream Offer

Brandon Hill

Table of Contents

PART IV: THE MOST COMMONLY ASKED QUESTIONS AND WHAT INTERVIEWERS ARE LOOKING FOR

- CAN YOU WALK US THROUGH YOUR RESUME?/CAN YOU TELL US A LITTLE ABOUT YOURSELF?
- WHY DO YOU WANT TO WORK FOR (INSERT FIRM)?
- WHAT HAVE YOU DONE THAT HAS PREPARED YOU FOR THIS POSITION?
- WHY SHOULD WE HIRE YOU OVER SOMEONE ELSE?
- WHERE DO YOU SEE YOUR CAREER IN FIVE YEARS?
- WHAT DO YOU LIKE TO DO IN YOUR FREE TIME?
- CAN YOU TELL US ABOUT A TIME YOU MADE A MISTAKE?
- HOW DO YOU HANDLE STRESS AND WORKING UNDER PRESSURE?
- WHAT ARE YOUR STRENGTHS?
- TALK ABOUT A TIME YOU WORKED IN A GROUP AND ENCOUNTERED A CONFLICT.

Preface

The information given in this short read has been accumulated from my personal experience and the working professionals I have been lucky enough to be exposed to in my young career. These include professors, career coaches, and employees in investment banking, Big 4 accounting, consulting, wealth management, hedge funds, and everything in between. These people I have been in contact with range from Interns all the way up to Partners, Managing Directors, and Fund Managers.

After going through the interviewing process countless times, I saw many things not being emphasized by typical articles, books or courses giving interviewing advice. A lot of the information was also outdated. In 2018, things are vastly different than they were a decade ago.

For firms, new methods and technologies are being used, and for students, there are new ways to study and prepare. Through my network of professionals, I was able to collect golden nuggets of information that I would like to share with those aspiring to work in the world of accounting or finance.

Out of respect for the professionals and firms I have acquired wisdom from, I will not be using the names of the individuals or the firms they were a part of. Instead, I will be referring to the "Knowledge Team" or "KT." Whenever you see that pop up in the text, know that it is real advice coming from one of the 15+ individuals in these industries.

I know how busy students can be during the interview season. One thing I always hated was a book with too much fluff and not enough substance. That's why I made this a 'no fluff' policy book. I want to give useful advice and actionable tips that you can implement right away to start improving your interviewing skills.

Part I: Foundation

1: The Skill of Interviewing

Year after year, it seems like the lives of business majors are becoming harder and more stressful as the landscape for internships or full-time offers becomes more competitive. Students are doing whatever they can to put themselves in a position to land their dream job.

Whether you are trying to work at a Big 4 accounting firm or a prestigious investment bank, there is a skill that can make or break your chances of being hired: interviewing. Nowadays, one can no longer get by from what's on their resume, and who you know can only take you so far. There is a sea of candidates for firms to choose from that all look worthy on paper. How they perform during their interview is what ends up being the deal breaker.

An Associate at an investment bank told me that students with 4.0's from great schools were being turned away over people with 3.5's from smaller schools. The deciding factors on choosing one over the other came down to their interviewing skills. Some might think that the 4.0 student could walk their way into a prestigious position, but it isn't that easy.

"An interview can show you a lot about a candidate that you just can't find out from their resume. You can see how they carry themselves, how they articulate their answers, what their personality is like, and if you can see them working with you for long hours."
- KT

Throughout this short read, there are tips and tactics on how to gain small advantages across the whole interviewing process. Isolated, each tip might seem to have no value, but when you add them up and execute, you'll be leaps and bounds ahead of your competition.

2: The Process of Interviewing

The process of interviewing can't begin unless you apply to the positions.

You will need to be on top of the dates and deadlines for every firm you have your eyes on. The bulk of interviews take place from August through October, which is a large period to keep track of. Look out for resources from your career center to find out when applications are due. Firms will also have this information on their website. Some firms only give you one day to apply for their program, so this is not something you will want to take lightly!

TIP: Much of your success during this process is being proactive and staying organized. Many candidates miss deadlines, forget about a campus event, and underestimate the time needed to prepare for an interview. By simply not messing these things up, you already have an edge over some of your peers.

After you apply, the process will usually begin in a few weeks with someone reaching out to you for the first interview. This can be a phone interview, online interview, or an in-person campus interview. It can be conducted by a recruiter, HR employee of the firm, or someone from the team you are interviewing for. This interview will typically be less than 20 minutes and is a way for the firm to gauge if you could be a fit for them. While most of them consist of get-to-know-you questions, some initial interviews can contain technical questions, so always be prepared.

TIP: Never take any interview lightly. Thorough research should always be done, even for a simple phone interview. During my junior year, I applied for a Financial Analyst intern program for a firm and had a recruiter reach out to me for the first call. I unwisely assumed that this interview would be a short call for the recruiter to get to know me and walk through my resume. I was completely caught off guard with multiple in-depth technical questions. From that point forward, I never assumed an interview would be easy.

If you are selected to continue, you'll be invited to a firm's Super Day, which is a day of multiple rounds of interviews at a firm. The interviewers will be from different teams and divisions ranging from recently entry-level employees all the way to upper management. The thought of it can be intimidating, but after you become a seasoned interviewer, it will not matter if you have one interview or ten that day. It will all feel the same to you.

On the evening before the Super Day, there may be a networking event everyone is invited to. It should be no surprise that this should be seen as mandatory for you. You'll be there for about an hour and a half, and it will begin with some HR representatives presenting to the group on the company and how the interview process will work.

After that, firm's will usually have some current employees talk to the group about their position and experience at the firm. Once they are done speaking, they will tell you that you are free to go and that they will stick around if you want to talk to them. Do not just leave!

This is your opportunity to ask these employees any questions you might have and gives you a chance to show your face to them. They may or may not be your interviewers, but if you make a good impression on them, you never know who they might tell. Be assertive while trying to speak to everyone because all the other candidates in the group will be doing the same...at least the candidates that didn't leave immediately after being dismissed.

Contact after the Super Day can be quick or can take a few weeks. I have been contacted with an offer hours after my final interview, and I have also been contacted more than two weeks after. The Knowledge Team says to be patient because there are a number of factors that influence the length of time from the first interview to the offer.

3: Types of Interview Questions

There are several types of questions that are asked in all interviews. Each of them is equally important and should be mastered by the time you are interviewing for your dream internship or full-time position. Some may come easier to you than others. For me, behavioral and fit questions always came naturally, but I struggled to grasp a few concepts on technical questions. Continue to practice the question types you are strong at, but really focus on those weaknesses.

Picture this. You are 25 minutes into an interview, and so far, you have been killing it. All of the questions have been fit or behavioral, and you have answered them correctly. You think you are in the clear until they hit you with a simple technical question that you do not know the answer to. You freeze up and see the interviewer give you a look of dissatisfaction before you have to say "I'm not sure."

This scenario can play out any number of ways. Maybe you did well in technicals but couldn't talk about the different ways JP Morgan makes money. No matter the combination, a lack of skill in any of the following question types will be exposed eventually and can put a dent on a great interview.

Behavioral

These questions are asked to gauge how you HAVE acted in certain situations or how you WOULD act in certain situations. When you formulate your answers, you want to be sure to use stories that took place in your professional life, not your everyday life. Employers are looking to see that you know how to handle certain situations that come up in the workplace. Those things could be encountering conflict, making a mistake, dealing with clients, and working under pressure.

All behavioral questions should be answered using the STAR (Situation Task Action Result) technique. If you have never heard of this method, it is quite simple.

For example, if an interviewer asked you "Can you talk about a time you made a mistake in the workplace?" you would answer by first explaining what the situation is.

"I was interning for a hedge fund during my sophomore year."

Then, you would explain the task.

"An analyst gave me a project to update the historical returns of the benchmark their fund was compared to. I had updated the amounts with the numbers and turned the report in before later realizing I had updated them with values from the HFRX and not the HFRQ index. Although the numbers were very similar, I knew that I had to tell the analyst I had made a mistake."

Finally, talk about the result.

"With an internship at a hedge fund, making a mistake was the last thing I wanted to do. Not telling the analyst would be detrimental to the accuracy of the reports submitted. I always hold myself accountable and live with the consequences. Thankfully, the analyst had not submitted the reports to his boss yet, and I was able to update the numbers with the correct index."

Try quizzing yourself with behavioral questions and practice using the STAR method.

Fit

Fit questions are asked to find out just that. Are you a good fit for the position, team, and company? While answering these questions, you want to be sure that you are sending this message to your interviewers. You should read the job descriptions in the applications to find the traits they are looking for. Use these traits or adjectives while you formulate your answers to fit questions.

Technical

If your interviews have a section of technical questions, this could be an area to show that you mean business. Technical questions will undoubtedly be asked for investment banking and consulting interviews. They may or may not be asked in other interviews.

You may be able to answer every technical question that is asked of you, but the ways you go about explaining them could affect how they are perceived. Some candidates are asked a technical question, and they spit out the answer that is memorized right out of every book that tells you how to answer "How are the financial statements linked together?"

In 2018, firms are aware of these books out there and what the answers say. Interviewers are not looking for someone who is good at memorizing facts. They are looking for someone who actually knows this information. Even if you are one of these people that memorized every question for a situation like this, there is a way to go about answering technical questions that can leave a good impression.

When you answer technicals, try to speak clearly and at a normal pace like you would in a conversation. Don't just quickly recite the answer like it was a game show. Look at both of your interviewers as you talk, and make sure you fully answer what they were asking. Leave the interviewers with the impression that you actually understand what you are talking about on a conceptual level.

Firm/Industry Knowledge

Interviewers like to know that you are serious about working for their firm. They want to feel that they are your number one option as an employer and that you are committed for the long-term. One way for them to do that is to ask questions about the firm or industry they are in.

You should be able to express why you want to work for PWC or what makes them different than EY. You should know all the ways that Goldman Sachs makes money and what their divisions are. Nothing feels better than being asked a tough question, answering it in depth, and seeing the positive reaction from the interviewer.

"We ask questions about the firm or the position they are applying for because we want to know if they are serious about it. It won't separate you from the rest by being able to answer a basic question like 'What does our company do?' Every person should be able to answer that. But if you can't, then we have a problem."
- 	KT

Case Studies

Case studies will definitely be a part of a consulting interview and are becoming more popular across accounting and investment banking firms. They are the ultimate way to test your knowledge because case interviews tie in aspects from several subjects you should have learned in your classes.

An interviewer will read the case aloud to you. You'll have time to digest what was said and to ask questions for clarification. From there you will think through the case and will try to come up with a solution. There is an endless number of books on strategies to answer case study questions. I would recommend you read one of them.

I will tell you that it is essential that you explain your thought process during a case interview. Don't compute or assume anything in your head without saying it aloud. You will likely struggle during some parts of a case question, and this is to be expected. The interviewers issue a case study to find out how your brain ticks. They can't do this if you remain silent and do things in your head.

"We have hired many people that weren't able to complete the case study. We did so because we saw that the person was bright, given the way they went about organizing all of the variables from the case and thinking through possible scenarios."
-    KT in Consulting

Current Events

I know investment banks love to bring this question type up in an interview. One reason is simple. They want to see if you follow the market and news to stay on top of the industry. The second reason is to test your knowledge beyond standard questions.

The professionals at these firms are smart, and they were in your position not too long ago. They know the average student is capable of memorizing how you get from "revenues" to "free cash flow." One way for them to truly test your knowledge is to ask you about some current events.

They may ask "Tell me about something you have heard in the news." You might reply with an answer mentioning how interest rates are set to rise again. If you were able to come up with some news, you are not in the clear yet. The interviewer may keep drilling down with follow-up questions.

Example:

Interviewer: "Tell me something you have heard recently in the news."

You: "Well, I was reading through the Wall Street Journal and saw that the Fed is considering another rate hike soon."

Interviewer:

"Why does the Fed adjust interest rates?"

"Why is now a good time?"
"How will this affect the economy?"
"What will this do to the price of bonds?"

They can take your simple answer and find a way to drill down to test your knowledge on several different topics. Whether you are interviewing at an accounting firm, banking firm, or somewhere else, you will want to make sure that you are staying up to date with what is happening.

Going into the interview, have a list of 3-5 current events that you could talk about extensively. Anticipate what their follow-up questions could be and have ready responses for those as well.

4: Interview Preparation

Once you land the interview, the hardest part of the process of getting an offer can either be over or about to begin. For me, I always felt that getting the interview was the hardest part. I wasn't from a target school and didn't have the best GPA out there, so when I made it to the Super Day, I felt like I was 75% there already. The cause behind this feeling was the confidence I had in my interviewing abilities.

If you get called in for the chance to interview, you should feel some sort of relief. You made it through the weed out process, and someone actually thinks you could work at their firm! That should be something to be excited about and should give your morale a boost. After a short pat on the back, it's time to buckle down to plan your preparation.

You have probably been to a career workshop or read an article on how to prepare for your interviews, but I'd like to offer some more in-depth advice that stems from the experience and knowledge of current working professionals who have recently gone through or administered this process many times.

Research

All great interviews begin with deep research. You should assume anything that could be asked WILL be asked in your interview. These are the 5 main areas I would focus on gathering research.

1. Position
2. Interviewers
3. Firm

4. Industry
5. Related current events

Position

Before you move onto the other four areas, you will want to make sure that you have as much information on the position as possible. You should know what the job description is and what qualifications the firm is searching for. Also, know what a typical day in the life is like for someone in that position.

Hopefully, you can find this information right off the firm's website. However, to go deeper and gather a thorough understanding, you will have to go the extra mile. Here are some ways to find more information.

- Search online forums
- Use your network to find someone who is currently in that position or a similar one
- Ask representatives at your career center on campus
- Watch informational YouTube videos

Interviewers

Finding information on your interviewers is not always something that is available, nor necessary. On a Super Day, it is likely you will not know the names of any of your interviewers beforehand. However, maybe you know that you are applying for a particular role or division. By researching those two areas, it will help you know a little about your interviewers too.

Firm

Knowing all about the firm you are applying for can benefit you in many ways. Not only will you be able to answer any questions thrown at you like...
- "Who are our competitors?"
- "What beliefs and values do our firm have?"
- "What products and services do we offer?"

But you will also be able to answer questions like...
- "Why do you want to work for us?"

- "What makes you think you are fit for this company?"
- "Where do you see yourself in 5 years?"

To acquire this knowledge, I would begin by browsing the firm's website, taking note of all the major things on it.
- Company overview
- Mission statement and values
- Divisions and departments
- Products and services offered
- Their blog and news page
- Key senior leadership

Following this, I would also suggest reading through the firm's annual report. You can learn a lot about their business model and financials from the annual report. You don't need to memorize the financials exactly, but you should have a general idea of them in case you need to talk about them.

Part of knowing about the firm you are interviewing for is understanding their competitors. Some interviewers might ask you "Who are our competitors?" or "What makes us different from our competitors?"

Create a table of 4-5 competitors to the firm you are applying for and jot down a few talking points for each of them. Find out what their highlights are and how that differs from the place you are applying at.

Industry

Having knowledge on the industry your firm is in will benefit you during the whole interview. If you are applying to an accounting firm, you will be able to answer "Why are our services important to a business?" If you are applying to an investment bank, you will be able to answer "Do you know what the working hours per week are for an Analyst position?"

By researching the industry, you will gain knowledge to help you think like the interviewer. Once you can think like them, you can give them the answer they want based off of what you know and have experienced. To learn about a certain industry, you can follow the same steps above for acquiring knowledge on the "position" and "firm."

Relevant Current Events

If you are in the business school of your university, you have certainly been advised to start reading the Wall Street Journal every day. Well, I am here to tell you that you need to be reading that, along with any other respectable news platforms.

Not only will this improve your interviews, but it will improve your life in general. Knowing what's going on in the world and how certain events affect the markets or economy is powerful. Aside from the Wall Street Journal, I also suggest having several apps such as CNBC, Bloomberg, and Yahoo Finance. Just browse through these apps for 10 minutes every day, and within a few weeks, you will surprise yourself with how much you learn.

Part II: Practice

5: Storytelling

Once you have accumulated research, you can think about how you will start answering questions in all the categories listed in Chapter 3. You'll want to try to craft stories for each of them. Storytelling is a skill within itself, and you have to become good at it to deliver a great interview.   Storytelling is important because...

- You can fully answer any type of question
- It gives you a chance to impress with your communication skills
- It allows you to show some of your personality through your answers

Being able to captivate your interviewer's interest with a great story is key to leaving a great impression. Here are some tips for you while you tell your stories.

 Be enthusiastic
- Keep your story thorough, but concise, as it is easy to ramble with unimportant information
- Have structure with your story. Have a beginning, middle, and ending. In the end, summarize and explain how that answers the question
- Always end stories on a positive note

6: Quizlet Flashcards

Quizlet might just be the greatest thing to happen to college students. If you went to school prior to them cracking down on their content, you have probably struck gold once or twice by finding the answers to study guides, homework assignments, and even exams.

Quizlet flashcards were also the primary way I studied for interviews. I would type out the potential interview question on the front and my answer on the back. I preferred to use Quizlet cards over traditional notecards because of the time it takes to create.

With traditional cards, it takes far too long to write out all the necessary cards. For my interviews with big investment banks, my flashcard deck could get up to 300 cards! I know that sounds like overkill. And it may well be. But when you are studying for your dream job, you want to have practiced any possible thing that could come up.

Let's get into how to create your study sets and how you should practice them.

First, I would research on Glassdoor to find out any unique questions that the firm is known for asking. Maybe they ask you to talk about the firm, or perhaps they always ask specific technical questions. Make a list of those questions and import them into Quizlet. Next, I would make notecards for all of the most popular questions known to be asked in the finance and accounting industry.

- "Tell me about yourself."
- "Why do you want to work for the firm?"
- "What have you done to prepare you for this position?"
- "What do you do in your free time?"

Once these are a part of your set, I suggest you Google to find lists of common "behavioral" and "fit" interview questions. These are a majority of the questions in these interviews, as the firm is trying to find out how you have acted in certain situations and if you would be a fit for the position and firm.

At this point, your set of notecards should have over 100 questions. I would then add any technical questions that could be asked. For a Big 4 accounting firm, they may ask you what certain line items mean or what type of journal entries would be made. For an investment bank, they might ask you to walk them through a Discounted Cash Flow analysis. I recommend adding questions like these to your set.

Finally, the last type of notecards I would make would be cards about the firm or the position. Look at the job posting and read the bullets of what they are looking for. You can create notecard questions based off of these bullets. If one of the requirements says "excellent Excel skills with financial modeling" you can create a card that says "How good are you at financial modeling?" If it is in the job posting, it will likely be asked about.

For notecards on the firm, I would research the main things to know about the company. You should know what their business is, the divisions they have, what they believe in and value, and any recent news on the firm. Interviewers want to gauge your interest, and this is one way for them to do that. Not being able to formulate an answer when someone asks "How do we make money?" will immediately give the impression that you weren't serious about the position.

Practicing With the Notecards

Once your notecards are created, practice them until you master them. Be sure to practice them with the "shuffle" mode selection. The great thing about practicing notecards on shuffle is that you cannot anticipate or remember what the next card could be. The current card could be a behavioral question, and the following card could be a question on the firm.

At this point in the studying, I would practice these questions until I had no issues with every card in the deck. To get to this point, don't just sit at a desk and read the questions and answers in your head. Speak the answers aloud as if it was the actual interview. This way, you can monitor how you are speaking and can make tweaks if necessary. Sit down and look out ahead of you while you practice, envisioning your interviewer in front of you. Ask yourself …

- How am I sitting right now?
- What am I doing with my hands?
- Am I loose and relaxed?
- Am I talking too fast?

After I feel that I have mastered this, I will practice the cards at different locations and different times of day to ensure that I have mastered the questions in any scenario.

7: Role-Play With Family or Friends

If you have a friend or roommate that you trust to give you honest and constructive feedback, set up some mock interviews with them. These are great because you can give them your Quizlet list and have them ask you the questions in any order. Not only can they ask you what was on the card, but encourage them to have follow-up questions to your mock answers. This will simulate the real deal. You can run a phone interview, a video interview, or a face to face interview.

By practicing any of the three, you will have the benefit of someone seeing or hearing things that you might not pick up on in your own practicing. Maybe you didn't realize you said "like" every three seconds. Perhaps you didn't realize you tap your foot during your answers.

You will need to set things straight with your interviewer before starting. Although you are friends, you want to have unbiased and blunt feedback. No sugarcoating. Let them know that they are doing you a disservice if they decide not to mention things that they notice, good or bad.

If you have a warm network of connections with people in the industry, you could ask them to conduct your mock interview. It is best to have someone who has been in the industry and knows how an interview goes. Reach out to someone you know and respectfully ask if you can have a little bit of their time.

TIP: *Record these mock interviews so you can analyze how you did after. You'll be able to pick up on more things that need improvement, especially your nonverbal communication.*

8: Mirror Practicing

If you found some areas where your body language was awkward, or you sounded monotone at times, practicing in front of a mirror is a great way to become fluid. Simply set a chair in front of the mirror in your restroom and pretend the sink is the interview table. You can practice your questions aloud and can see how certain gestures and postures will look.

Practice what you want to do with your hands that will feel comfortable. Maybe have both hands on the "table" or maybe only one hand. Also, see what you look like with both hands in your lap. You'll find yourself in the interview using all three positions. By practicing in the mirror, you will be able to tell when those feel most comfortable.

9: Pomodoro Method

This method of time management has been popularized quite a bit in the recent decade. If you are unaware of it, this method involves doing a task for 25 minutes and taking a short break before repeating that process again. By doing these shorter intervals, you would theoretically get more done and be more attentive in your work.

The Pomodoro Method works great for practicing with interviews. Just practice your questions for 25 minutes and step away for a break before practicing again. The 25-minute intervals will allow you to stay energized and focused so you can practice for a longer time. Practicing questions for four hours straight without a break will wear you down, and you won't retain the information.

Stepping away for the break allows your mind to be off of the questions you are studying. Once you come back and practice those same questions, it gives your brain a chance to recall that information again. This spaced repetition has been shown by studies to be one of the most effective ways to absorb information into your long-term memory. The more times you have to recall the information, the better your chances are for remembering in the future.

10: Taking All Interviews You Can

If you look at major events in life where someone has to perform at their best, they never start at the highest level. An athlete doesn't jump straight to the championship game. And a student doesn't just take the final exam.

There are important events or competitions before that allow that person to have their abilities tested. Through this, they can become comfortable and grow under pressure. The same can be done for interviewing.

Practicing with notecards, watching YouTube videos, and conducting mock interviews with your peers is great, but can never replicate the pressure that is felt in an actual interview. Sure, you know how to sell yourself as a candidate when you are comfortable and have been practicing for hours. Do you really know how you would perform if the interview for your dream job was right now? You shouldn't wait until that interview comes to be prepared.

One method of preparation that I believed helped me most was interviewing as much as possible, for any position with any company. My peers that I interviewed confirmed that this was a big part of their success as well.

Beginning my sophomore year, I began to apply and interview for as many positions and firms as possible. One, I was actually trying to land my first internship. Two, I knew that interviews made me nervous and that I needed to practice them.

Soon enough, I began to get selected for interviews for a variety of positions. I went in knowing that most of them were not positions that I wanted, nor the career paths I wanted to take. However, I practiced for dozens of interviews and eventually found a process and made a template for my interviews.

This template looked like

1. Study the job posting and tailor my resume to it
2. See if any interview questions were on Glassdoor
3. Research who the interviewers were
4. Create every possible question you think could be asked as a Quizlet notecard

Because I was continually interviewing, I became desensitized to the fear and anxiety that is usually felt during an interview. I had been in those high-stress and high-pressure situations so many times that my comfort zone grew to where I wasn't intimidated anymore. Had I never done that, I believe I would have froze in an actual interview that mattered.

Even with all that practice, I still found myself feeling slightly anxious going into a big interview. It may never entirely go away when the time matters, but it can be subdued. When you are going into an interview for your number one option, you think to yourself "This moment right here can decide how my career path and life will pan out." That thought can overwhelm you, but by using this method of preparation, you can have that thought, recognize it, and rise to the occasion and kill it!

TIP: Fake it till you make it. When I first began interviewing, I was new to the business school and didn't have the slightest relevant work experience. I didn't have any connections or family in the industries I wanted to get into. Because of this, I felt less equipped than my peers that I was up against.

When I went into interviews, I would treat it as an acting performance. I would act like I was someone who had been there before. Someone who had the credentials and knowledge to get that position. Thinking of it as a performance helped take my mind off my self-consciousness.

11: A Little Housekeeping

Grooming and Appearance

As I have said before in this book, firm's have thousands of qualified candidates out there that are capable of filling their open positions. Exceptional grooming and appearance is something that can add a little to your case as a potential hire, but be a big detriment if you lack it. As much as we would like to believe that people don't judge books by their covers, it still happens.

First impressions are powerful, and if you can make a good one from the first sight AND deliver a great interview, things will be looking bright.

Social Media

This is something that you should already know, but it should be stressed again. Employers are increasingly looking at candidates' social media to look at how they present themselves online and if there are any red flags. You should never be posting questionable content to begin with, but if you post things that you wouldn't want an employer to see, keep your profile on private.

For your profile picture, don't have the photo be one of you taking a chug out of a huge liquor bottle. Keep a nice photo to represent yourself.

TIP: Emails used for your social media should not be the same emails that you use for applications. Part of the firm's process of finding you on social media is by searching your email on the platforms.

LinkedIn

Your LinkedIn profile will be viewed most by employers, and this is your chance to show that you mean business and a chance for you to toot your own horn. First and foremost, you should have a clean and professional profile picture. Normally seen as a minute detail, a nice LinkedIn profile picture is sort of just a checkbox item while reviewing a profile. If you have one, that's great. Mostly everyone does. But if you don't have one, it can raise a question on how seriously you take the platform and yourself. Employers want to hire people who will present themselves well because they will also be representing the firm.

Have your relevant work history entered in as well as your duties and responsibilities for those positions. Basically, have the information that is on your resume on your LinkedIn as well.

12: The Phone Interview

Phone Interviews can happen at different times during the interviewing process. Usually, a phone interview is the first contact you will have with a firm. This call is no longer than 20 minutes and is used to get to know you and see if you would be a good fit.

They will ask you to tell them about yourself, why you want to work for the firm, and why you would be a good fit for the position. While these interviews are usually conducted by HR representatives, it is not always the case and is no reason to take it lightly.

Phone interviews can also happen after your Super Day interview. Many times, employees of the firm at other locations want to get to know you as well since you could be interacting with them a lot if hired.

Whether it is either of these scenarios, the phone interview should be taken seriously, as you only have the option of making a good impact with your words and your voice. In an in-person interview, you can make a good impression by your appearance, your handshake, and with your body language. In a phone interview, realize that the person on the other side can't use their other senses to judge you.

Of course the content of what you're saying should have quality, but you should also focus on how you are talking. You should be...

- Speaking with volume and certainty
- Changing the tonality of your voice to avoid sounding like a robot
- Monitoring the speed at which you talk
- Aware that you are not using fillers such as "like" or "um"

TIP: *When conducting a phone interview, do so in a brightly lit room, and stand up on your feet during the call. Both of these will help with your energy levels, and that will show through on the other end of the phone.*

DOUBLE TIP: *Have your resume out, and the job description pulled up on your computer screen. The interviewer can't see you, so why not take advantage of having those materials in front of you? Ideally, you should have been prepared by that point, but have those there as a safety net in case you get stuck on a question.*

13: Online Video Interviews

Standard Video Call

The first is your standard video call with you on one side and your interviewer(s) on the other side of the camera. Be aware of the things you would keep track of in a typical interview such as your appearance, body language, and voice. You'll also need to ensure that your video setup is sufficient. Make sure you have the following:

-   The camera is eye-level with you so you are looking straight into the lens and not up or down at it. Use books or a box to elevate your laptop.
-   Have excellent lighting so your interviewers can see you clearly.
-   Make sure you have a clean backdrop. It doesn't have to be a plain white wall, but if there are things in your backdrop, ensure that nothing would be distracting to the interviewer.
-   Record a video of yourself and play it back to check the audio. You will want to make sure there is no echo.

Video Interviewing Vendor

With this type of video call, you will be on a third-party platform online. You will be given a link that will take you to the interview. Once you begin, you will be asked several questions total. For each question, a video will come up with someone from the firm asking you a question.

Following this, you will have 30 seconds to craft your response and your recording time will begin. You will usually have around three minutes to answer your question fully. After that, this process will repeat until you have answered all the questions.

Speaking into the small front-facing camera of your laptop can be awkward because you do not have someone to look at and receive immediate feedback from with their facial expressions and body language. In a face-to-face interview, an interviewer's facial expressions or nodding can let you know that you are on the right track with your response. Without this luxury in a digital interview, you will have to be hyper-aware of what you are saying and how you are saying it.

I didn't know this until I had already had about five of these interviews under my belt, but these recordings are far more than that. You are not merely being judged by what you are saying, but you are being analyzed in a variety of ways.

These video interviewing vendors are using artificial intelligence to rank you as a candidate. Your words, body language, appearance, and sound are all being analyzed and compared to previous "star" candidates. Firms are able to look at the interviews of previous exceptional candidates that went on to have success and can tell the AI to find them candidates with the same traits.

When I found this out, I was blown away. From that point on, I made sure that I did everything correctly. Here are some flash tips on how to appear like a desirable candidate.

- Have the camera at eye level, so you are not looking up or down into the camera
- Have proper lighting
- Make sure there isn't an echo resonating in the room
- Don't wear glasses if you can see there is a glare coming off
- Sit up straight, with your shoulders back to emit confidence
- Keep eye contact with the camera lens, not with your recording on the screen. Also, break eye contact with the lens appropriately, like you would talking to an actual person
- Speak with volume and a tone of certainty with your answers

- Don't keep your hands out of the recording the whole time. Stay loose and feel free to use your hands to express what you are saying and give off confident body language. Just don't overdo it.
- Have a personality while you answer. It's okay to smile and have other facial expressions. It will give you a chance to show you aren't a boring robot and that you are personable.

TIP: Mastering this takes practice. One good way to do it is to open up your Photo Booth app or something equivalent and record a mock interview on it. Practice some questions and answer how you would if it were real. You'll be shocked on how much you notice watching the recording after. Take notes and repeat the process until you are ready to go.

14: Knowing What Not To Do In An Interview

Here is a quick list of reminders of things that you should not do in an interview.

Don't...
- Chew gum
- Tap your foot
- Cross your arms
- Ask about vacations, salary, or how many hours you'll work
- Keep eye contact 100% of the time
- Try to outdress the employees there
- Bash previous peers, colleagues, employers, or the firm's competition
- Use unprofessional words, terms, or slang
- Be too passive or too aggressive
- Bring up religious or political views
- Interrupt someone speaking
- Lie about experience or accomplishments
- Be dull and boring while you talk

Part III: Execution

15: The Night Before and Day of the Interview

A little bit of preparation and planning can save you a lot of potential trouble before the interview. If it is the night before, you should have planned and practiced enough to avoid the need to study until 3:00 am. Be in bed at a time that allows you to get a good night's sleep. This is not the time you want to pull an all-nighter. A lack of sleep will be detrimental to the functioning of your brain, and your appearance can be affected too. Bloodshot eyes and dark bags under your eyes won't be a good look to your interviewers.

The night before should be for planning. Make sure you have your outfit picked out for the interview and that everything has been dry cleaned and ironed. You'll also want to plan out what time you are going to leave your house to head to the interview. Don't make any assumptions that you will have enough time. Plan to get to the interviewing site an hour early. The worst that could happen is that you have to sit there for an hour. If that is the case, it will be the perfect time to pull up the Quizlet app for additional reviewing.

Have your folder or messenger bag ready with your materials in it. You should have several copies of your resume, printed on high-quality resume paper. Also, bring your portfolio of work and anything else that you would find necessary for an interview. If transcripts are required, pack them the night before.

Day Of

Depending on what time your interview or Super Day starts, you can use the morning to practice over the most popular questions asked. Have your answer to "Walk us through your resume." down.

Morning Workout

If my interviews ever began at 11:00 am or later, I made sure that I went to the gym beforehand. By the day of the interview, I had practiced so much that I didn't need those extra two hours to study. What I did need was the added benefit exercise could have for my day.

Exercising is shown to relieve stress and tension in the body, which can help you settle down during the interviews. Also, the biggest reason I exercised before my interviews was to have positive endorphins released and blood flow rushed through my brain. Completing a morning workout left me feeling refreshed, awake, and put me in a confident mood going into the interviews.

Food & Nutrition

When it comes to food, everyone's body will be different. For morning interviews, some like to have a big breakfast. Some like to have a small breakfast. And some don't like to eat at all. If your interview is later in the afternoon, I would recommend having food in your system so you can function properly.

With your choice of food, choose options that you know resonate well with your body. Choose foods that will allow you to think clearly without an upset stomach or brain fog. A 3-entree meal from Panda Express two hours before your interview might not be the best option.

Go With What You Know

Don't try anything that you wouldn't normally do or are not accustomed to. Sure you want to be energetic for your interview, but if you have never had a 20-ounce Red Bull before, your interview is not the right time to try it. Doing things out of YOUR ordinary can cause distractions for you when it counts.

Before you head out to your interview, do a last minute double check that you have everything you need and that you look professional. Ensure your clothes are clean, free of any dog hair, lint, or small stains from coffee or anything else.

Be sure your shoes are shined and neat. Ensure that your belt, tie, and shoes all match. This is a small detail, but employers may unintentionally lookout for something like that. If you have the little things done correctly, you will make a great impression.

16: Bringing a Portfolio of Work With You

This is a major tip I picked up from a friend in college that I credit to be the reason I landed my first internship. It is a simple and extremely effective way to impress your interviewers and stand out.

Whenever you go into an interview, gather some projects or presentations you have worked on during your classes. For myself, I always kept a copy of this massive accounting project everyone had to do in our business school. The behemoth group project took over 80 hours of work and helped us in learning the different skills in financial accounting.

Since it was an extensive task for a group of three people, a lot of problems came about over the course of the semester. These events are usually ones that I bring up during "behavioral" interview questions.

For example, let's say the interviewers told you "Tell us about a time you dealt with conflict in a group."

I would usually reply with something like "Okay, during my sophomore year, we were assigned this large accounting project. We were to take a list of 60 raw transactions and perform different aspects of accounting to eventually create an annual report for this fictional company. With our group of three, we struggled to find time to coordinate schedules and found ourselves frustrated…."

I said this in an interview, and later, one interviewer said "Tell us more about this accounting project. What was it exactly that you were working on?"

My eyes lit up, and I replied "Oh! I actually brought it with me. Let me walk you through it."

Once I saw their initial reaction, I knew I had just found a golden nugget for interviewing. I let them go through the spiral bound annual report, and they were blown away. From that point on, I always brought a portfolio of work with me and probably brought it out in three out of every four interviews I had after that.

For an interviewer, it is great when a candidate can tell you about their qualifications or experience, but when one can show their actual work, it immediately boosts credibility and sense of professionalism. For any position you are applying for, look back at the work you have done and see if it could be something that you could bring out in an interview to help your case.

17: Know Your Resume and Background

Interviewing is mostly knowing how to talk about yourself and what you have accomplished. It is easier said than done, but one way to help you improve on it is to fully know what is on your resume. You shouldn't just know the bullet points you typed out, but you should be able to talk about them in depth if you were asked to. For every club you joined, you should be able to talk about what the club's purpose was and how you participated in it. For any previous internship or job, you should be able to talk about what you did and how you made an impact.

Under your "Experience" section, if you listed that you increased sales at your company by 15%, you better be able to explain how you got to that number. In every interview, you will be asked to "walk" your interviewers through your resume or explain your background.

As you answer these questions, think about what the interviewers are looking for and tie your story into that. For an investment banking internship, you can talk about how your extracurriculars gave you the knowledge and professional skills required for the position. For a consulting job, you can explain how you won a case competition you took part in and how that experience sparked your desire to become a consultant.

By knowing what you have done inside and out, you can think quicker on your feet during the interview to tailor your responses to what they are looking for.

18: The Interview Starts Once You Walk In

You are not just being judged during the time you are face to face with your interviewer. Many companies take the chance to judge your character and behavior from the second you walk into the building.

Your interactions with the receptionist may be relayed to hiring managers. The way you sit in the waiting room could also be watched.   Are your feet up on the coffee table? Are you slouching and chewing obnoxiously on a piece of gum?

Or are you sitting upright, professionally, giving the impression that you are ready for business? Be aware of these possibilities and don't let your guard down. Treat everyone you encounter with respect and kind manners.

19: Waiting to be Called

Once you are at the firm and checked in, the waiting you do leading up to your interview can be an overwhelming time if you allow it to be. As you wait, you may begin to feel nervous and have some anxiety. You are not the only one to feel this way. In fact, a majority, if not all, of the other candidates are going to feel this as well.

Your breath may shorten, the heart will race, and you will begin to sweat. This is your flight or fight mechanism kicking in. It is an evolutionary response when your body senses that it is in a dangerous situation. Why would that be happening right now before an interview? Well, your mind sees the interview as something that is intimidating and dangerous. The idea that your career path is on the line and you are about to be judged is being perceived as life-threatening by your body.

Once you recognize this mechanism and that it is normal, you can do things to calm yourself down. The most effective way to do this is by controlling your breathing. By breathing slowly, you are telling your body that things are fine and that it can settle down.

A simple deep breathing method called "box breathing" can be performed. With box breathing, you want to inhale four seconds, pause four seconds, exhale four seconds, and pause four seconds. Those four steps create the "box," and you can repeat that until you are settled down.

Once you are calm, check to make sure that your hands aren't all sweaty. We have all heard how important the first handshake is and having a sweaty hand from being nervous will ruin that first moment between you and your interviewer.

Lastly, double check that your cell phone is on silent. If you are wearing a smartwatch, make sure it is on silent and that the vibration haptic is turned off as well.

20: First Impressions

Your name can be called by an HR representative or one of your interviewers. Either way, you should treat everyone with equal respect. I don't need to talk about the importance of a firm handshake because you should know that by now. However, there are additional things that can add to that moment where you walk in and shake your interviewers' hand.

Walk in with your back straight up and shoulders pushed back. Don't overdo this or you'll end up looking like those tools at the gym that think they are jacked. Just do this enough so you send out confident energy with your body language. Greet your interviewer or interviewers with a smile on your face.

If there is more than one interviewer, shake the woman's hand first. As you shake their hand, give a simple "Hi, I'm _____, it is great to meet you."

TIP: Remember the interviewers' names as you meet each other. To help with this, repeat their name aloud back at them as you shake their hand and repeat it in your head several times. You will want to use their names as the interview wraps up and you thank them and leave.

After shaking their hands, don't sit down until you are offered a seat. If you aren't verbally offered a seat, wait until your interviewers sit for you to sit down. One of my KT mentors mentioned how he picks up on the smallest manners from candidates during interviews and how it leaves a good impression on him about their character.

21: Learn to Think Like the Interviewer

A significant aspect of the skill of interviewing is knowing how to think like an interviewer. After reading through countless job descriptions and interviewing consistently for years, I started to feel like I cracked the code of interviewing. Once I got into my professional life and sat on the other side of the interview table, I was able to see when candidates had this as well.

Some candidates would give us the answer we were looking for while others would leave us scratching our heads because they would reply with an answer that raised a red flag. They would say they just wanted the job "as a stepping stone to a better firm." Or "I'd prefer to not work long hours." This may be surprising to you, but it still happens, and the Knowledge Team has experienced this during the final rounds of prestigious interviews.

"I don't know if candidates aren't reading the job descriptions, or don't know what they're getting into, or what? But once a red flag comes up in an interview, it is hard for them to recover and build a case that they are still the one we want."
    -KT

You have to learn to tell your interviewers what they want to hear. This is NOT the same as lying to make sure you check all their boxes for qualifications. You should learn how to take your own experiences and gained knowledge to craft the answer that they are looking for.

As the interview is going on, feel out the situation and adjust your answers and body language if necessary. Interviewers are all different, and some prioritize things more than others. Look for any cues that they might give off. If one of them leans in attentively while you are discussing a major project you worked on, it'd be a good idea to keep explaining what you did. This, along with cues like nodding and facial expressions can tell you that you have their interest.

What Can YOU do for THEM?

While expressing your answers, always be saying things that show what you can do for THEM. Deep down they don't care what the job or position can do for you. In the end, it is a business, and the business is there to make money and create value for shareholders. They want to know if you are going to benefit them, their teams, and the firm as a whole. Keep this in mind as you answer. Some quotes I like to throw into any of my answers are…

- "…and I really think that these traits and experiences will transfer over well into this position to bring value to your team."
- "…I'd love to have a long career at this firm and would hope to move up over the years, wherever I am needed to bring the most value."
- "….because I have done ___, ___, and ___, I believe that I am the best candidate and can bring the most value to your team and firm."

I definitely use a quote like one of these to conclude my response to the "Tell me about yourself" question, but they are also used in nearly every "Fit" question type. So while you create your stories to practice the various "Fit" questions, see how you can include quotes in them to tell your interviewers how you can be valuable.

22: Being Concise

Rambling on for a few minutes for every question is detrimental to your interview. By going on and on you are...

- Losing your interviewer's attention
- Giving yourself less time to answer other questions they had
- Showing weakness in your communication skills

Answer your questions fully, but don't go overboard.

TIP: *Don't panic or become self-conscious when you see the interviewer writing on your resume. It happens for every candidate. These interviewers see a few dozen candidates in a short period of time and can't remember everyone. When they write on your resume, they are taking notes on your interview, so they have something to refer to during the selection process.*

23: Stress Tests

Stress tests don't come up in every interview, but you are bound to come across one at some point. This is a way for interviewers to try to throw you off in the middle of an interview to see how you react to adverse conditions.

My most memorable stress test was for a Financial Analyst Program for a tech company. The interview was going completely normal up to the stress test. My interviewer was a friendly man, and the conversation was going well. As I began to answer one question, he repeatedly said "Okay. Okay. Okay. Okay" while I was giving him my response. He had to have said the word at least 30 times during my answer. It threw me off for a split second, but I was able to remain focused and clearly explain my answer.

After that, the interview was back to normal for a few minutes. As he asked me a question, he gave me a dead and lifeless stare for what seemed like an eternity. As I was answering, he kept this stare and didn't even blink, let alone move his body. This threw me off more than the first test because it felt like I was talking to a brick wall.

Stress tests come in various forms, including...

- Stern staring
- Good cop, bad cop with multiple interviewers
- Aggressive questions
- Interrupting your answers
- Reasking of questions
- Playing devil's advocate for any of your responses

If you come across any of these, recognize what is happening and keep your cool. Stay focused, and deliver your answer.

24: Verbal and Nonverbal Communication

During the course of an interview, the interviewers are obviously there to learn about you, see if you're competent, and if you could be an asset to the firm. Aside from the content of what you say, interviewers are collecting information and judging you on numerous verbal and nonverbal cues. Some of these are picked up because of human nature, and other things are intentionally sought out for during your interview.

Verbal

While you are replying to questions asked by the interviewers, keep in mind that you are sending them certain messages with how you conduct your speech.

1. Speed of Voice
    a. The speed at which you talk should be monitored. Be aware if you are talking too fast. This can send the message that you are nervous and can throw off the interviewer from the things you are actually saying.
    b. On the other hand, speaking too slow can lull the interviewers to sleep. The best way to go about this is to speak at a pace that allows you to get your message across while keeping your interviewers listening.
2. Tonality and Volume
    a. The tonality of your voice is the pitch that you are speaking at. If you were to speak at the same tonality, you would be called monotone and would sound like a robot. If you listen to any good speaker, they change up the tonality of their voice to help send a certain message.
    b. By changing the tonality and volume in your interview, you can keep the attention of your

interviewers better and can get your message across clearer. Use your tonality and volume to emphasize what you find important.

Nonverbal

I'm sure at some point, you have heard a crazy statistic on what percentage of communication is nonverbal. I have seen numbers of 50%, 70%, and up to 93%. To be conservative, let's say that 50% of communication is nonverbal. This is still a considerable amount, and the Knowledge Team professionals I interviewed have confirmed that they analyze a candidate's nonverbal communication throughout the interviewing process.

1) Upright posture
2) Eye contact with both interviewers
3) Appropriate use of hands and gestures
4) Mirroring the body language of your interviewers

Nearly everyone I have talked to from Analyst up to Managing Director agrees that poor body language in an interview affects their opinion of a candidate. This may sound shallow. You might be thinking that they should judge someone off of their background, resume, and what they are verbally saying. I would agree with you, but you have to understand that these prestigious firms have thousands of qualified candidates to choose from. Anything that can be docked will be docked.

"A candidate that speaks well, with enthusiasm, and with the right body language, makes an immediate impression on me as an interviewer. I can tell the person is a professional and it helps me remember them at the end of the day when we are deciding who we want to hire."
- KT, Senior Associate

While Your Interviewers are Speaking

Your body language while you are not speaking is equally important to be aware of. While your interviewers are speaking, keep eye contact with them, but don't stare the entire time. Nod your head in agreement to things that are said to show you are listening. Maintain great posture and have your shoulders and hands relaxed.

Throughout the entire interviewing process, you want to ask yourself "What message am I sending right now?" You want to send the message that you are competent, coachable, dedicated, and personable. If you have made it to the final rounds of the interviews, these people have already established that it is reasonable that you are good enough to work for them. With these positions, it is likely that you are going to be working long hours. The interviewers want to know if they can see themselves spending a significant amount of time with you. They don't want someone that could be cancerous to their team.

What to do in Between Interviews on your Super Day

Once your first interview of the day is done, you'll find that a significant amount of nervousness and pressure has disappeared from you. While preparing for your next interview, you want to do what you can to remain comfortable. Drink some water to make sure you are hydrated and that your mouth isn't dry. Use the restroom and also check your appearance in the mirror to make sure everything is tidy. Check your tie knot, hair, nostrils, mouth corners, and any other areas. After that, there isn't anything else to it. Stay relaxed and ready for the next interview.

25: The End of the Interview

Do you have any questions for us?

This question is asked in every interview, and it can add to your case as a candidate if done correctly. It is good to have a handful of questions going into the interview that you would like to ask. I wouldn't plan on asking more than three questions because it would take too much time from your interviewers.

Ask thoughtful questions. Don't dig up some fun fact from their annual report and say "I noticed five years ago that revenues were down 6%. Why was that?" This isn't going to impress the interviewer and it will annoy them. No one likes the try hard during interviews.

A question like "What are some of the reasons you like working for Deloitte?" would be more appropriate. It gets the interviewer talking about themselves and shows you are interested in the firm.

One I personally liked to ask and got good responses from was "What are some things a person new to this position would have to learn to get caught up to speed at the firm?" Asking a question like this will send the message that you are proactive, coachable, and willing to learn.

TIP: Your interviewers will likely tell you about their background and what they do in the firm. Take note of what they say as the interview goes on. Sometimes, when the interview finishes and they ask "Do you have any questions?" I bring up something that they said.

For example, if they talked about how they were an engineering major in college and ended up switching to a double major in finance and accounting, I would ask them about it. A question from me could be like "You said you started off as an engineering major. What made you make the decision to change and why did you choose finance and accounting?"

People love to talk about themselves, and this will show that person that you have excellent listening skills.

What's Next?!

When you finish asking your prepared questions, they will ask you "Any other questions?" The final thing you will want to ask is "What are the next steps from here?"

This will allow them to explain to you how the rest of the process will play out and what the timeline will be before a decision is made.

Thank You and Goodbye

You did it! The worst is over, and you made it through the interview. One final touch to leave a lasting impression is to thank your interviewers and shake their hands. Remember what their names were, and as you shake their hand, say "Thank you ____" with their name. It's something small, but something only a small percentage of candidates do.

TIP: If the interviewers hand you a business card, don't just grab it and put it in your pocket. People find this disrespectful. They take pride in their business cards, and you should feel lucky to be extended one. When handed a card, look at it and read it for a few seconds before putting the card away. It is a respectful gesture.

26: Follow Up and Thank-You Notes

This is an area I never personally took advantage of. With the interviews I was in, it never felt necessary for me to send a thank-you note to my interviewers. However, when I was interviewing candidates to replace me as an intern at a firm, one candidate hand wrote a thank-you letter to me, and it left a meaningful impression.

That candidate had a great interview with us, but so did a few other ones as well. This thank-you letter was short, simple, and effective. It left me with the impression that he was a professional and would go above and beyond to get the job done.

I asked a Vice President at a banking firm what he thought about thank you letters, and he said this...

"Thank-you letters can be great, or they can be annoying. I like letters that are short. Probably only a few sentences. Other letters consisted of a few paragraphs and were full of kiss-ass material. I didn't like that at all."
-     KT

So with that, I would suggest writing thank-you letters to your interviewers if you feel that it is right. If you write one, keep it short. Basically, say..

-     Thank you for the time
-     You appreciate the opportunity
-     Reaffirm your interest for the position and company

That's all it takes. The act of giving the handwritten card will have far more impact than what was written on it. Don't write a novel kissing up and begging for the position. That immediately turns interviewers off.

Conclusion

There are many subtle aspects of interviewing that individually, may seem irrelevant, but when put together, are noticed by interviewers and help separate you from the rest. That's what this whole book was about. Do the little things correctly, and the results can be huge.

The landscape nowadays for these prestigious internships or full-time offers are hypercompetitive, and everyone is looking for the slightest edge against the other candidates.

It's easy to read some of the tips in this book and say "Come on! People are really looking at that and holding it against us?!" Although you may find some of it nitpicky, this judgment does happen, and you want to maximize your chances of standing out by implementing what you have learned in this short read.

The strategies and tactics from this book are useless if they are not applied through practice first. You won't be able to learn to think like an interviewer if you have not been face to face with one numerous times. Take what you have learned here and practice again and again. Find out what your comfort zone is, and push past that as many times as possible. Seek out tough interviews and tough feedback from people. It won't feel pleasant, but it WILL help you in the end.

This book was written after a lot of research and trial and error. My goal is to help others by shortening this learning curve to help them get their dream offer. Hopefully, this will have that impact on you. Go out there, be confident, and be a go-getter! The opportunities are yours for the taking.

Part IV: The Most Commonly Asked Questions and What Interviewers are Looking For

Can you walk us through your resume?/Can you tell us a little about yourself?

This will be the first question asked in an interview 95% of the time. Your interviewers know nothing about you aside from what is listed on your resume. Even if they did have your resume beforehand, they might not have caught every detail that was on there.

Before going into the interview, answering this question should be second nature to you. You should have practiced your response to perfection because this is one of the most critical points of the interview. Everyone has a different way of creating their response to this, but I will list out some things that you need to address somewhere in your answer.

- A short background of who you are
- Why you chose your school and major
- Extracurriculars you participated in
- What lead you to choose that career path
- Previous work experience
- What you learned and accomplished from your extracurriculars and work experience
- How the above has given you the skills, knowledge, and confidence to be an asset to the firm

Why do you want to work for (insert firm)?

This question would be categorized as "fit." The interviewers want to know your reasoning behind wanting to work for their firm. Do you actually want to work for them, or do you just want the big paycheck?

When you answer this question, think about what the interviewers want to hear. They want to hear that...

- You have a genuine interest in the position and industry
- Their firm is your number one choice
- Your previous experience prepared you for that career path
- You have a good idea of what's expected.
    - You could get this information online or from meeting a current employee at an info session
- You want to be there for the long-term

With these things in mind, think about how you could talk about your knowledge, skills, and experience to hit those several marks.

What have you done that has prepared you for this position?

If you didn't address this in your "Walk me through your resume" answer, you might be asked this. Before the actual interview, you should have practiced this question on a Quizlet notecard. During the research process, you should have found out what the position is and what it implies.

If there was a job description on the posting, you want to take note of everything they are looking for. Watch YouTube videos and browse the internet to find out all you can. Once you know what the position requires, you can create your answer using your experience to make sure you hit everything they are looking for. You could say that you...

- have had internships that relate to the position
- learned hard skills and soft skills through your extracurriculars that will transfer over into the position
- took every elective and workshop you could to prepare you for a career in that industry
- have talked to several mentors to find out what the job is like. Through that, you knew you would be a perfect fit.

Why should we hire you over someone else?

With this question, the interviewers want to know why you are different. Every candidate they interview has had some level of success to get to that point. If everyone is great, why should they hire you?

Think about things that set you apart from the pack. Don't say that you work harder than everyone else, SHOW them you do through past experiences that would reflect that. If you feel that you have unique skills or experience, explain them here.

TIP: Whatever adjectives you use to describe yourself needs to be backed up by concrete evidence. This is where having your physical portfolio of work can come in handy. You'll have actual evidence of a project you worked on and showing this can validate your credibility.

Pick three things that you believe separates you from the rest. As you answer, explain each of the three individually and why that makes you the best candidate. After explaining your third reason, summarize them all, so your interviewer has a clear understanding of what you said.

Where do you see your career in five years?

Firms like to ask this "fit" question to get a feel of what your plans are for the near future. Your answer will allow them to form an opinion on if you are right for the position. They are looking to find answers to the following questions...

- What are your motives for the position?
- Do you know what you're getting into?
- Are you just going to be there for a few years and leave?
- Do you have a clear vision of your career path?
- Are you willing to do what it takes to work your way up?

Also be sure to convey the message that you...

- Want to add value to the firm in any way possible
- Are looking to learn and develop as a professional
- Want to succeed by any means

Avoid saying things like...

- "I'd like to use this position as a stepping stone to a better one."
- "I see myself working in this division for a year or two before I try to transfer to a different one."
- "I plan on being here for a few years before going off to grad school."

Although these are great aspirations to have, they aren't the ideal answers to this question.

What do you like to do in your free time?

This is an easy question, but candidates still find a way to mess this up. When you tell someone what you like to do, you should bring up things that have positive connotations with them. These are activities like...

- Going to the gym
- Traveling and being outdoors
- Creating art
- Reading books

Activities like these send messages to interviewers that you possess traits that could translate over into the position. Going to the gym could imply that you care about yourself and that you have discipline and structure. Creating art can show them that you have a passion for the work you put out. And reading books can communicate that you are curious and willing to learn.

Things to avoid saying you do include...
- Binge watching Netflix
- Playing video games till 3:00 am
- Getting drunk at the bars on the weekends

The interviewers will hear these activities and might associate them with being reckless and undisciplined. These activities aren't necessarily bad. We are all human and enjoy these things every now and then. Just don't mention it for this question. Remember, always be aware of how your words will be perceived.

Can you tell us about a time you made a mistake?

During my undergraduate years, workshops, books, and articles all told us to practice the "What are your weaknesses?" question. Out of my personal experience of interviews, I was only asked that question once. I asked a Knowledge Team member if firms still asked that question and she said...

"Nahh. No one really asks that question anymore because we know that everyone has prepared for it. We try to throw them off with something else."

I asked her what they asked in replacement, and it was this question right here. By asking when someone made a mistake, they are testing the same things as when they ask a candidate for a weakness. Interviewers ask these questions to find out...

- if you are honest with yourself
- if you hold yourself accountable
- If you made the decision the improve or resolve the issue and how you did it

Be sure to cover these three areas in your response. Use the STAR method that was mentioned earlier in the book. The situation and task can be your explanation of what your mistake was and how you made it. The action will be how you went about addressing and resolving the issue, and the result will be what happened in the end.

As you wrap up your answer, do so in a way that leaves the interviewer feeling positive about what you said. Talk about what you learned, why you were glad you held yourself accountable, and how you benefited from that experience from that point on.

How do you handle stress and working under pressure?

This question is mostly a "behavioral" question, but also a bit of "fit." Interviewers are looking to see how you work under these conditions. They want to find out how you go about keeping your cool and performing when things aren't going smoothly. Based on your answer, they could get a good idea on if you fit in with the firm.

It can't be stressed enough. You have to think like the interviewer! No interviewer is going to want to hear that you are afraid of stress and pressure or don't deal with it well. You want to find a good example in your past that put you under true stress. Don't choose to talk about a situation that might not be perceived as stressful.

Examples of situations you could find stories for include...

- High stake projects
- Short time constraints
- Being overloaded with work
- Being asked things beyond your skills and knowledge
- Having conflicts with group members

Once you have an idea of what you are going to say, use the STAR method to explain. Again, always end on a positive note.

What are your strengths?

This question is similar to the "Why should we hire you over someone else?" question in the sense that you are trying to separate yourself from the pack with your answer. Interviewers want to know what your strengths are to see if they fit with the position and team. From this, they can see what benefits you could bring to the table. Most of the advice I have on this question is what NOT to say. You should stay away from basic answers that everyone says such as...

- "I'm a hard worker"
- "I've wanted to work in this industry since I was a little kid"
- "I'm smart"

A man from the Knowledge Team was telling me how often candidates use these vague and boring responses to answer these questions. He says that these answers can be expressed in ways that don't involve these phrases. His advice included...

- Reading job descriptions or websites to find out what they are looking for
- Having your strengths be a few of those things
- Backing up what you say with proof

I would add to this with a reminder to always mention how your strengths could be valuable to the position and team.

Talk about a time you worked in a group and encountered a conflict.

A high percentage of interviews will include this question. It is mostly a "behavioral" question, but also "fit." When you prepare for this question, you should look at your answer and ask yourself "What does this story show them about my behavior?"

In this question, interviewers are listening for certain things to come up with an opinion on how you behave in a group setting and what your personality is like. They are looking to see if you...

- Handle conflict in a responsible and calm manner
- Hold yourself and others accountable
- Have the ability to put yourself in someone else's shoes to understand their side
- Have positive leadership qualities
- Take on an extra load to solve the issue
- Can come up with resolutions to fix the issue

They do not want to hear that you...

- Blame others for the conflict
- Boss people around in your group
- Let the rest of your group resolve the conflict

Use the STAR method and your storytelling abilities to form your answer. Think of any big group projects you have done in school or have worked on in a job or an internship.

The interviewers ultimately want to know if you are someone that can work well with others and still get the job done if a conflict arises. In the workplace, group conflicts always pop up with time constraints, conflicting personalities, opposing opinions, and differences in work styles.